About the Autho…

Ted Hughes was … famous writers ar… for 14 years. T… means that he was recommended to the Queen to write poems for important events.

He grew up in West Yorkshire, where his father ran a local newsagent and his mother was famous for her jams and gooseberry pies.

As a child, he enjoyed spending time fishing and hunting with his brother in the countryside and rivers near his home. He loved the outdoors and a lot of his writing was inspired by nature.

Ted wrote his first poem at 15 years old and continued to write until his death in 1998. During this time, he wrote 20 books for children, of which his most famous was *The Iron Man*.

To Frieda and Nicholas

The Iron Man

Ted Hughes

Illustrated by Andrew Davidson

Published by Pearson Education Limited, Edinburgh Gate, Harlow, Essex, CM20 2JE.

www.pearsonschools.co.uk

Designed and typeset by Crow Books

First published Faber and Faber Limited in 1968. This educational edition first published by Pearson Education Limited in 2014.

17 16 15 14
10 9 8 7 6 5 4 3 2 1

British Library Cataloguing in Publication Data
A catalogue record for this book is available from the British Library

ISBN 978 0 435 16051 7

Printed in Slovakia by Neografia

Acknowledgements
Every effort has been made to contact copyright holders of material reproduced in this book. Any omissions will be rectified in subsequent printings if notice is given to the publishers.

This is a special edition of this book for Wordsmith.
To order further copies please contact:
Telephone: 0845 630 22 22
Fax: 0845 313 77 77
Email: customer.orders@pearson.com
Web: www.pearsonprimary.co.uk/wordsmith

CONTENTS

1
The Coming of the Iron Man

The Iron Man came to the top of the cliff.

How far had he walked? Nobody knows. Where had he come from? Nobody knows. How was he made?

Nobody knows.

Taller than a house, the Iron Man stood at the top of the cliff, on the very brink, in the darkness.

The wind sang through his iron fingers. His great iron head, shaped like a dustbin but as big as a bedroom, slowly turned to the right, slowly turned to the left. His iron ears turned, this way, that way. He was hearing the sea. His eyes, like headlamps, glowed white, then red, then infra-red, searching the sea. Never before had the

Iron Man seen the sea.

He swayed in the strong wind that pressed against his back. He swayed forward, on the brink of the high cliff.

And his right foot, his enormous iron right foot, lifted – up, out, into space, and the Iron Man stepped forward, off the cliff, into nothingness.

CRRRAAAASSSSSSH!

Down the cliff the Iron Man came toppling, head over heels.

CRASH!

CRASH!

CRASH!

From rock to rock, snag to snag, tumbling slowly. And as he crashed and crashed and crashed

His iron legs fell off.

His iron arms broke off, and the hands broke off the arms.

His great iron ears fell off and his eyes fell out.

His great iron head fell off.

All the separate pieces tumbled, scattered, crashing, bumping, clanging, down on to the rocky beach far below.

A few rocks tumbled with him.

Then

Silence.

Only the sound of the sea, chewing away at the edge of the rocky beach, where the bits and pieces of the Iron Man lay scattered far and wide, silent and unmoving.

Only one of the iron hands, lying beside an old sand-logged washed-up seaman's boot, waved its fingers for a minute, like a crab on its back. Then it lay still.

While the stars went on wheeling through the sky and the wind went on tugging at the grass on the cliff-top and the sea went on boiling and booming.

Nobody knew the Iron Man had fallen.

Night passed.

Just before dawn, as the darkness grew blue and the shapes of the rocks separated from each other, two seagulls flew crying over the rocks. They landed on a patch of sand. They had two chicks in a nest on the cliff. Now they were searching for food.

One of the seagulls flew up – Aaaaaark! He had seen something. He glided low over the sharp rocks. He landed and picked something up. Something shiny, round and hard. It was one of the Iron Man's eyes. He brought it back to his mate. They both looked at this strange thing. And the eye looked at them. It rolled from side to side looking first at one gull, then at the other. The gulls, peering at it, thought it was a strange kind of clam, peeping at them from its shell.

Then the other gull flew up, wheeled around and landed and picked something up. Some awkward, heavy thing. The gull flew low and slowly, dragging the heavy thing. Finally, the gull dropped it beside the eye. This new thing had five legs. It moved. The gulls thought it was a strange kind of crab. They thought they had found a strange crab and a strange clam. They did not know they had found the Iron Man's eye and the Iron Man's right hand.

But as soon as the eye and the hand got together the eye looked at the hand. Its light glowed blue. The hand stood up on three fingers and its thumb, and craned its forefinger like a long nose. It felt around. It touched the eye. Gleefully it picked up the eye, and tucked it under its middle finger.

The eye peered out, between the forefinger and thumb. Now the hand could see.

It looked around. Then it darted and jabbed one of the gulls with its stiffly held finger, then darted at the other and jabbed him. The two gulls flew up into the wind with a frightened cry.

Slowly then the hand crept over the stones, searching. It ran forward suddenly, grabbed something and tugged. But the thing was stuck between two rocks. The thing was one of the Iron Man's arms. At last the hand left the arm and went scuttling hither and thither among the rocks, till it stopped, and touched something gently. This thing was the other hand. This new hand stood up and hooked its finger round the little finger of the hand with the eye, and let itself be led. Now the two hands, the seeing one leading the blind one, walking on their finger-tips, went back together to the arm, and together they tugged it free.

The hand with the eye fastened itself on to the wrist of the arm. The arm stood up and walked on its hand. The other hand clung on behind as before, and this strange trio went searching.

An eye! There it was, blinking at them speechlessly beside a black and white pebble. The seeing hand fitted the eye to the blind hand and now both hands could see. They went running among the rocks. Soon they found a leg. They jumped on top of the leg and the leg went hopping over the rocks with the arm swinging from the hand that clung to the top of the leg. The other hand clung on top of that hand. The two hands, with their eyes, guided the leg, twisting it this way and that, as a rider guides a horse.

Soon they found another leg and the other arm. Now each hand, with an eye under its palm and an arm dangling from its wrist, rode on a leg separately about the beach. Hop, hop, hop, they went, peering among the rocks. One found an ear and at the same moment the other found the giant torso. Then the busy hands fitted the legs to the torso, then they fitted the arms, each fitting the other, and the torso stood up with legs and arms but no head. It walked about the beach, holding its eyes up in its hands, searching for its lost head. At last, there was thc head – eyeless, earless, nested in a heap of red seaweed. Now in no time the Iron Man had fitted his head back, and his eyes were in place, and everything in place except

for one ear. He strode about the beach searching for his lost ear, as the sun rose over the sea and the day came.

The two gulls sat on their ledge, high on the cliff. They watched the immense man striding to and fro over the rocks below. Between them, on the nesting ledge, lay a great iron ear. The gulls could not eat it. The baby gulls could not eat it. There it lay on the high ledge.

Far below, the Iron Man searched.

At last he stopped, and looked at

the sea. Was he thinking the sea had stolen his ear? Perhaps he was thinking the sea had come up, while he lay scattered, and had gone down again with his ear.

He walked towards the sea. He walked into the breakers, and there he stood for a while, the breakers bursting around his knees. Then he walked in deeper, deeper, deeper.

The gulls took off and glided down low over the great iron head that was now moving slowly out through the swell. The eyes blazed red, level with the wavetops, till a big wave covered them and foam spouted over the top of the head. The head still moved out under water. The eyes and the top of the head appeared for a moment in a hollow of the swell. Now the eyes were green. Then the sea covered them and the head.

The gulls circled low over the line of bubbles that went on moving slowly out into the deep sea.

2

The Return of the Iron Man

One evening a farmer's son, a boy called Hogarth, was fishing in a stream that ran down to the sea. It was growing too dark to fish, his hook kept getting caught in weeds and bushes. So he stopped fishing and came up from the stream and stood listening to the owls in the wood further up the valley, and to the sea behind him. Hush, said the sea. And again, Hush. Hush. Hush.

Suddenly he felt a strange feeling. He felt he was being watched. He felt afraid. He turned and looked up the steep field to the top of the high cliff. Behind that skyline was the sheer rocky cliff and the sea. And on that skyline, just above the edge of it, in the dusk, were two green lights. What were two green lights doing at the top of the cliff?

Then, as Hogarth watched, a huge dark figure climbed up over the cliff-top. The two lights rose into the sky. They were the giant figure's eyes. A giant black figure, taller than a house, black and towering in the twilight, with green headlamp eyes. The Iron Man! There he stood on the cliff-top, looking inland. Hogarth began to run. He ran and ran. Home. Home. The Iron Man had come back.

So he got home at last and gasping for breath he told his dad. An Iron Man! An Iron Man! A giant!

His father frowned. His mother grew pale. His little sister began to cry.

His father took down his double-barrelled gun. He believed his son. He went out. He locked the door. He got in his car. He drove to the next farm.

But that farmer laughed. He was a fat, red man, with a fat, red-mouthed laugh. When he stopped laughing, his eyes were red too. An Iron Man? Nonsense, he said.

So Hogarth's father got back in his car. Now it was dark and it had begun to rain. He drove to the next farm.

That farmer frowned. He believed. Tomorrow, he said, we must see what he is, this iron man. His feet will have left tracks in the earth.

So Hogarth's father again got back into his car. But as he turned the car in the yard, he saw a strange thing in the headlamps. Half a tractor lay there, just half, chopped clean off, the other half missing. He got out of his car and the other farmer came to look too. The tractor had been bitten off – there were big teeth-marks in the steel.

No explanation! The two men looked at each other. They were puzzled and afraid. What could have bitten the tractor in two? There, in the yard, in the rain, in the night, while they had been talking inside the house.

The farmer ran in and bolted his door.

Hogarth's father jumped into his car and drove off into the night and the rain as fast as he could, homeward.

The rain poured down. Hogarth's father drove hard. The headlights lit up the road and bushes.

Suddenly – two headlamps in a tall treetop at the roadside ahead. Headlamps in a treetop? How?

Hogarth's father slowed, peering up to see what the lights might be, up there in the treetop.

As he slowed, a giant iron foot came down in the middle of the road, a foot as big as a single bed. And the headlamps came down closer. And a giant hand reached down towards the windshield.

The Iron Man!

Hogarth's father put on speed, he aimed his car at the foot.

Crash! He knocked the foot out of the way.

He drove on, faster and faster. And behind him, on the road, a clanging

clattering boom went up, as if an iron skyscraper had collapsed. The iron giant, with his foot knocked from under him, had toppled over.

And so Hogarth's father got home safely.

BUT

Next morning all the farmers were shouting with anger. Where were their tractors? Their earth-diggers? Their ploughs? Their harrows? From every farm in the region, all the steel and iron farm machinery had gone.

Where to? Who had stolen it all?

There was a clue. Here and there lay half a wheel, or half an axle, or half a mudguard, carved with giant toothmarks where it had been bitten off. How had it been bitten off? Steel bitten off?

What had happened?

There was another clue.

From farm to farm, over the soft soil of the fields, went giant footprints, each one the size of a single bed.

The farmers, in a frightened, silent,

amazed crowd, followed the footprints. And at every farm the footprints visited, all the metal machinery had disappeared.

Finally, the footprints led back up to the top of the cliff, where the little boy had seen the Iron Man appear the night before, when he was fishing. The footprints led right to the cliff-top.

And all the way down the cliff were torn marks on the rocks, where a huge iron body had slid down. Below, the tide was in. The grey, empty, moving tide. The Iron Man had gone back into the sea.

SO

The furious farmers began to shout. The Iron Man had stolen all their machinery. Had he eaten it? Anyway, he had taken it. It had gone. So what if he came again? What would he take next time? Cows? Houses? People?

They would have to do something.

They couldn't call in the police

or the Army, because nobody would believe them about this Iron Monster. They would have to do something for themselves.

So, what did they do?

At the bottom of the hill, below where the Iron Man had come over the high cliff, they dug a deep, enormous hole. A hole wider than a house, and as deep as three trees one on top of the other. It was a colossal hole. A stupendous hole! And the sides of it were sheer as walls.

They pushed all the earth off to one side.

They covered the hole with branches and the branches they covered with straw and the straw with soil, so when they finished the hole looked like a freshly-ploughed field.

Now, on the side of the hole opposite the slope up to the top of the cliff, they put an old rusty lorry. That was the bait. Now they reckoned the Iron Man would come over the top of the cliff out of the sea, and he'd see the old lorry which was painted red, and he'd come down to get it to chew it up and eat it. But on his way to the lorry he'd be crossing the hole, and the moment he stepped with his great weight on to that soil held up only with straw and branches, he would crash through into the hole and would never get out. They'd find him there in the hole. Then they'd bring the few bull-dozers and earth-movers that he hadn't already eaten, and they'd push the pile of earth in on top of him, and bury him for ever in the hole. They were certain now that they'd get him.

Next morning, in great excitement, all the farmers gathered together to go along to examine their trap. They came carefully closer, expecting to see his hands tearing at the edge of the pit. They came carefully closer.

The red lorry stood just as they had left it. The soil lay just as they had left it, undisturbed. Everything was just as they had left it. The Iron Man had not come.

Nor did he come that day.

Next morning, all the farmers came again. Still, everything lay just as they had left it.

And so it went on, day after day. Still the Iron Man never came.

Now the farmers began to wonder if he would ever come again. They began to wonder if he had ever come at all. They began to make up explanations of what had happened to their machinery. Nobody likes to believe in an Iron Monster that eats tractors and cars.

Soon, the farmer who owned the red lorry they were using as bait decided that he needed it, and he took it away. So there lay the beautiful deep trap, without any bait. Grass began to grow on the loose soil.

The farmers talked of filling the hole in. After all, you can't leave a giant pit like that, somebody might fall in. Some stranger coming along might just walk over it and fall in.

But they didn't want to fill it in.

It had been such hard work digging it. Besides they all had a sneaking fear that the Iron Man might come again, and that the hole was their only weapon against him.

At last they put up a little notice:

DANGER:
KEEP OFF

to warn people away, and they left it at that.

Now the little boy Hogarth had an idea. He thought he could use that hole, to trap a fox. He found a dead hen one day, and threw it out on to the loose soil over the trap. Then towards evening, he climbed a tree nearby, and waited. A long time he waited. A star came out. He could hear the sea.

Then – there, standing at the edge of the hole, was a fox. A big, red fox, looking towards the dead hen.

Hogarth stopped breathing. And the fox stood without moving – sniff, sniff, sniff, out towards the hen. But he did not step out on to the trap. Slowly, he walked around the wide patch of raw soil till he got back to where he'd started, sniffing all the time out towards the bird. But he did not step out on to the trap. Was he too smart to walk out there where it was not safe?

But at that moment he stopped sniffing. He turned his head and looked towards the top of the cliff. Hogarth, wondering what the fox had seen, looked towards the top of the cliff.

There, enormous in the blue evening sky, stood the Iron Man, on the brink of the cliff, gazing inland.

In a moment, the fox had vanished.

Now what?

Hogarth carefully quietly hardly breathing climbed slowly down the tree. He must get home and tell his father. But at the bottom of the tree he stopped. He could no longer see the

Iron Man against the twilight sky. Had he gone back over the cliff into the sea? Or was he coming down the hill, in the darkness under that high skyline, towards Hogarth and the farms?

Then Hogarth understood what was happening. He could hear a strange tearing and creaking sound. The Iron Man was pulling up the barbed-wire fence that led down the hill. And soon Hogarth could see him, as he came nearer, tearing the wire from the fence posts, rolling it up like spaghetti and eating it. The Iron Man was eating the barbed fencing wire.

But if he went along the fence, eating as he moved, he wouldn't come anywhere near the trap, which was out in the middle of the field. He could spend the whole night wandering about the countryside along the fences, rolling up the wire and eating it, and never would any fence bring him near the trap.

But Hogarth had an idea. In his pocket, among other things, he had a long nail and a knife. He took these out. Did he dare? His idea frightened him. In the silent dusk, he tapped the nail and the knife blade together.

Clink, Clink, Clink!

At the sound of the metal, the Iron Man's hands became still. After a few seconds, he slowly turned his head and the headlamp eyes shone towards Hogarth.

Again, Clink, Clink, Clink! went the nail on the knife.

Slowly, the Iron Man took three

strides towards Hogarth, and again stopped. It was now quite dark. The headlamps shone red. Hogarth pressed close to the tree-trunk. Between him and the Iron Man lay the wide lid of the trap.

Clink, Clink, Clink! again he tapped the nail on the knife.

And now the Iron Man was coming. Hogarth could feel the earth shaking under the weight of his footsteps. Was it too late to run? Hogarth stared at the Iron Man, looming, searching towards him for the taste of the metal that had made that inviting sound.

Clink, Clink, Clink! went the nail on the knife. And

CRASSSHHH!

The Iron Man vanished.

He was in the pit. The Iron Man had fallen into the pit. Hogarth went close. The earth was shaking as the Iron Man struggled underground. Hogarth peered over the torn edge of the great pit. Far below, two deep red headlamps glared up at him from the pitch blackness. He could hear the Iron Man's insides grinding down there and it sounded like a big lorry grinding its gears on a steep hill. Hogarth set off. He ran, he ran, home – home with the great news. And as he passed the cottages on the way, and as he turned down the lane towards his father's farm, he was shouting "The Iron Man's in the trap!" and "We've caught the Iron Giant."

When the farmers saw the Iron Man wallowing in their deep pit, they sent up a great cheer. He glared up towards them, his eyes burned from red to purple, from purple to white, from white to fiery whirling black and red, and the cogs inside him ground and screeched, but he could not climb out of the steep-sided pit.

Then under the lights of car headlamps, the farmers brought bulldozers and earth-pushers, and they began to push in on top of the

struggling Iron Man all the earth they had dug when they first made the pit and that had been piled off to one side.

The Iron Man roared again as the earth began to fall on him. But soon he roared no more. Soon the pit was full of earth. Soon the Iron Man was buried silent, packed down under all the soil, while the farmers piled the earth over him in a mound and in a hill. They went to and fro over the mound on their new tractors, which they'd bought since the Iron Man ate their old ones, and they packed the earth down hard. Then they all went home talking cheerfully. They were sure they had seen the last of the Iron Man.

Only Hogarth felt suddenly sorry. He felt guilty. It was he, after all, who had lured the Iron Man into the pit.

3
What's to be Done with the Iron Man?

So the Spring came round the following year, leaves unfurled from the buds, daffodils speared up from the soil, and everywhere the grass shook new green points. The round hill over the Iron Man was covered with new grass. Before the end of the summer, sheep were grazing on the fine grass on the lovely hillock. People who had never heard of the Iron Man saw the green hill as they drove past on their way to the sea, and they said: "What a lovely hill! What a perfect place for a picnic!"

So people began to picnic on top of the hill. Soon, quite a path was worn up there, by people climbing to eat their sandwiches and take snaps of each other.

One day, a father, a mother, a little boy and a little girl stopped their car and climbed the hill for a picnic. They had never heard of the Iron Man and they thought the hill had been there for ever.

They spread a tablecloth on the grass. They set down the plate of sandwiches, a big pie, a roasted chicken, a bottle of milk, a bowl of tomatoes, a bagful of boiled eggs, a dish of butter and a loaf of bread, with cheese and salt and cups. The father got his stove going to boil some water for tea, and they all lay back on rugs munching food and waiting for the kettle to boil, under the blue sky.

Suddenly the father said: "That's funny!"

"What is?" asked the mother.

"I felt the ground shake," the father said. "Here, right beneath us."

"Probably an earthquake in Japan," said the mother.

"An earthquake in Japan?" cried the little boy. "How could that be?"

So the father began to explain how an earthquake in a far distant country, that shakes down buildings and empties lakes, sends a jolt right around the earth. People far away in other countries feel it as nothing more than a slight trembling of the ground. An earthquake that knocks a city flat in South America, might do no more than shake a picture off a wall in Poland. But as the father was talking, the mother gave a little gasp, then a yelp.

"The chicken!" she cried. "The cheese! The tomatoes!"

Everybody sat up. The tablecloth was sagging in the middle. As they watched the sag got deeper and all the food fell into it, dragging the tablecloth right down into the ground. The ground underneath was splitting and the tablecloth, as they watched, slowly folded and disappeared into the crack, and they were left staring at a jagged black crack in the ground. The crack grew, it widened, it lengthened, it ran

between them. The mother and the girl were on one side, and the father and the boy were on the other side. The little stove toppled into the growing crack with a clatter and the kettle disappeared.

They could not believe their eyes. They stared at the widening crack. Then, as they watched, an enormous iron hand came up through the crack, groping around in the air, feeling over the grass on either side of the crack. It nearly touched the little boy, and he rolled over backwards. The mother screamed. "Run to the car," shouted the father. They all ran. They jumped into the car. They drove. They did not look back.

So they did not see the great iron head, square like a bedroom, with red glaring headlamp eyes, and with the tablecloth, still with the chicken and the cheese, draped across the top of it, rising out of the top of the hillock, as the Iron Man freed himself from the pit.

When the farmers realized that the Iron Man had freed himself they groaned. What could they do now? They decided to call the Army, who could pound him to bits with anti-tank guns. But Hogarth had another idea. At first, the farmers would not hear of it, least of all his own father. But at last they agreed. Yes, they would give Hogarth's idea a trial. And if it failed, they would call in the Army.

After spending a night and a day

eating all the barbed wire for miles around, as well as hinges he tore off gates and the tin cans he found in ditches, and three new tractors and two cars and a lorry, the Iron Man was resting in a clump of elm trees. There he stood, leaning among the huge branches, almost hidden by the dense leaves, his eyes glowing a soft blue.

The farmers came near, along a lane, in cars so that they could make a quick getaway if things went wrong. They stopped fifty yards from the clump of elm trees. He really was a monster. This was the first time most of them had had a good look at him. His chest was as big as a cattle truck. His arms were like cranes, and he was getting rusty, probably from eating all the old barbed wire.

Now Hogarth walked up towards the Iron Man.

"Hello," he shouted, and stopped. "Hello, Mr Iron Man."

The Iron Man made no move. His eyes did not change.

Then Hogarth picked up a rusty old horseshoe, and knocked it against a stone: Clonk, Clonk, Clonk!

At once, the Iron Man's eyes turned darker blue. Then purple. Then red. And finally white, like a car headlamps. It was the only sign he gave of having heard.

"Mr Iron Man," shouted Hogarth. "We've got all the iron you want, all the food you want, and you can have it for nothing, if only you'll stop eating up the farms."

The Iron Man stood up straight. Slowly he turned, till he was looking directly at Hogarth.

"We're sorry we trapped you and buried you," shouted the little boy. "We promise we'll not deceive you again. Follow us and you can have all the metal you want. Brass too. Aluminium too. And lots of old chrome. Follow us."

The Iron Man pushed aside the boughs and came into the lane. Hogarth joined the farmers. Slowly they drove back down the lane, and slowly, with all his cogs humming, the Iron Man stepped after them.

They led through the villages. Half the people came out to stare, half ran to shut themselves inside bedrooms and kitchens. Nobody could believe their eyes when they saw the Iron Man marching behind the farmers.

At last they came to the town, and there was a great scrap-metal yard. Everything was there, old cars by the hundred, old trucks, old railway engines, old stoves, old refrigerators, old springs, bedsteads, bicycles, girders, gates, pans – all the scrap iron of the region was piled up there, rusting away.

"There," cried Hogarth. "Eat all you can."

The Iron Man gazed, and his eyes turned red. He kneeled down in the yard, he stretched out on one elbow. He picked up a greasy black stove and chewed it like a toffee. There were delicious crumbs of chrome on it.

He followed that with a double-decker bedstead and the brass knobs made his eyes crackle with joy. Never before had the Iron Man eaten such delicacies. As he lay there, a big truck turned into the yard and unloaded a pile of rusty chain. The Iron Man lifted a handful and let it dangle into his mouth – better than any spaghetti.

So there they left him. It was an Iron Man's heaven. The farmers went back to their farms. Hogarth visited the Iron Man every few days. Now the

517

Iron Man's eyes were constantly a happy blue. He was no longer rusty. His body gleamed blue, like a new gun barrel. And he ate, ate, ate, ate – endlessly.

4
The Space-Being and the Iron Man

One day there came strange news. Everybody was talking about it. Round eyes, busy mouths, frightened voices – everybody was talking about it.

One of the stars of the night sky had begun to change. This star had always been a very tiny star, of no importance at all. It had shone up there for billions and trillions and sillions of years in the Constellation of Orion, that great shape of the giant hunter that strides across space on autumn and winter nights. In all its time this tiny star had never changed in any way.

Now, suddenly, it began to get bigger.

Astronomers, peering through their telescopes, noticed it first. They watched it with worried frowns.

That tiny star was definitely getting bigger. And not just bigger. But bigger and Bigger and BIGger. Each night it was BIGGER.

Bigger than the Dog-star, the large, coloured twinkler at the heel of the Hunter Orion.

Bigger than Jupiter, the great blazing planet.

Everybody could see it clearly, night after night, as it grew and Grew and GREW. They stared up with frightened faces.

Till at last it hung there in the sky over the world, blazing down, the size of the moon, a deep, gloomy red. And now there could be only one explanation. That star was getting bigger because it was getting nearer. And nearer and NEARer and NEARER.

It was rushing towards the world.

Faster than a bullet.

Faster than any rocket.

Faster even than a meteorite.

And if it hit the world at that speed,

why, the whole world would simply be blasted to bits in the twinkling of an eye. It would be like an Express train hitting a bowl of goldfish.

No wonder the people stared up with frightened faces. No wonder the astronomers watched it through their telescopes with worried frowns.

But all of a sudden – a strange thing! The star seemed to have stopped.

There it hung, a deep and gloomy red, just the size of the moon. It got no smaller. It got no bigger. It wasn't coming any nearer. But it wasn't going away either.

Now everybody tried to explain why and how this was. What had happened? What was happening? What was going to happen?

And now it was that the next strange thing occurred – the astronomers noticed it first.

In the middle of the giant star, a tiny black speck had appeared. On the second night this speck was seen to be wriggling, and much bigger. On the

DAILY NEWS
ALL STARS FADE
SPACE DRAGON NEARER

third night, you could see it without a telescope. A struggling black speck in the centre of that giant, red, gloomy star.

On the fifth night, the astronomers saw that it seemed to be either a bat, or a black angel, or a flying lizard – a dreadful silhouette, flying out of the centre of that giant star, straight towards the earth. What was coming out of the giant star?

Each night, when the astronomers returned to their telescopes to peer up, this black flying horror was bigger. With slow, gigantic wing-beats, with long, slow writhings of its body, it was coming down through space, outlined black against its red star.

Within a few more nights, its shape had completely blotted out the red star. The nameless, immense bat-angel was flying down at the earth, like a great black swan. It was definitely coming straight at the earth.

It took several days to cover the distance.

Then, for one awful night, its wings seemed to be filling most of the sky. The moon peered fearfully from low on the skyline and all the people of earth stayed up, gazing in fear at the huge black movement of wings that filled the night.

Next morning it landed – on Australia.

BARRRUMP!

The shock of its landing rolled round the earth like an earthquake, spilling teacups in London, jolting pictures off walls in California, cracking statues off their pedestals in Russia.

The thing had actually landed – and it was a terrific dragon.

Terribly black, terribly scaly, terribly knobbly, terribly horned, terribly hairy, terribly clawed, terribly fanged, with vast indescribably terrible eyes, each one as big as Switzerland.

There it sat, covering the whole of Australia, its tail trailing away over Tasmania into the sea, its foreclaws on the headlands of the Gulf of Carpentaria. Luckily, the mountains and hills propped its belly up clear of the valleys, and the Australians could still move about in the pitch darkness, under this new sky, this low queer covering, of scales. They crowded towards the light that came in along its sides. Of course, whoever had been on a mountain-top when the dragon landed had been squashed flat. Nothing could be done about them. And there the horror sat, glaring out over the countries of the world.

What had it come for? What was going to happen to the world now this monstrosity had arrived?

Everybody waited. The newspapers spoke about nothing else. Aircraft flew near this space-bat-angel-dragon, taking photographs. It lay over Australia higher than any mountains, higher than the Hindu Kush in Asia, and its head alone was the size of Italy.

For a whole day, while the people of the earth trembled and wept and prayed to God to save them, the space-bat-angel-dragon lay resting, its chin sunk in the Indian Ocean, the sea coming not quite up to its bottom lip.

But the next morning, early, its giant voice came rumbling round the world. The space-bat-angel-dragon was speaking. It wanted to be fed.

And what it wanted to eat was – living things. People, animals, forests, it didn't care which, so long as the food was alive. But it had better be fed quickly, otherwise it would roll out its tongue longer than the Trans-Siberian railway, and lick huge swathes of life off the surface of the earth – cities, forests, farmlands, whatever there was. It would leave the world looking like a charred pebble – unless it were fed and fed quickly.

Its voice shook and rumbled around

the earth for a whole hour as it delivered its message. Finally it ended, and lay waiting.

The peoples of the world got together. If they fed it, how could they ever satisfy it? It would never be full, and every new day it would be as hungry as ever. How can you feed a beast the size of Australia? Australia is a vast land, all the countries of Europe will fit easily into Australia. The monster's stomach alone must be the size of Germany.

No, they would not feed it. The people of the world decided they would not feed this space-bat-angel-dragon or whatever it was – they would fight it. They would declare war on it, and all get together to blast it off the face of the earth. And so it was that all the peoples of earth declared war on the monster, and sent out their armed forces in a grand combined operation.

What a terrific attack!

Rockets, projectiles of all sorts,

missiles and bombs, shells and flame-throwers – everything was tried. The smoke of the explosions drifted out over the Pacific like a black, crawling continent. The noise of the battle shook the world almost as much as the landing of the dragon had done, and for much longer.

Then the noise died down and the smoke cleared. And the peoples of the world cried in dismay. The dragon was actually smiling. Smiling! Aircraft flying daringly near photographed the vast face smiling, and the picture was in all the papers.

It was smiling as if it had been well tickled.

Now the peoples of the world were worried. They were all great fighters. All spent their spare money on preparing for wars, always making bigger and better weapons, and now they had all tried their utmost to blast this thing off the earth, and what was the result?

The dragon merely smiled, and not

a scratch could be seen anywhere on its body.

Human weapons had no effect on it.

But that wasn't surprising. This creature had come from the depths of space, out of the heart of a star. Nobody knew what it was made of. Perhaps it could not be destroyed by any means whatsoever.

And now the space-bat-angel-dragon spoke again.

It gave the peoples of the world one week in which to prepare its first meal.

They could prepare what they liked, said the dragon. But if the meal was not ready in a week, then he would start on the cities and the towns.

The peoples of the earth, the kings, the Presidents and Ministers, the farmers and the factory workers and the office workers began to lament. Now what would happen to them? They would like to say the monster didn't exist, but how could they? There it was, covering Australia, staring out over all the countries of the world.

Now the little boy Hogarth heard all about this.

Everybody in the world was talking about it, worrying about it.

He was sure the Iron Man could do something. Compared to the space-bat-angel-dragon the Iron Man wasn't very big, of course. The Iron Man was only the size of a tall tree. Nevertheless, Hogarth had faith in the Iron Man.

He visited the Iron Man in his scrap-yard, and talked to him about this great monster that was threatening the earth.

"Please," he asked, "please can't you think of some way of getting rid of it? If you can't, then it's the end of us all."

The Iron Man chewed thoughtfully at his favourite titbit, a juicy, spicy old gas-stove. He shook his head slowly.

"Please think of something," cried Hogarth. "If this space-bat-angel-dragon licks all life off the earth, that'll be the end of your scrap iron – there'll be no people left to make it."

The Iron Man became still. He seemed to be thinking. Suddenly his headlamps blazed red, green, blue and white all at once. And he stood up. In a great grinding voice, he gave his commands. Hogarth danced for joy. The Iron Man had had the most stupendous idea. The Iron Man would go out, as the champion of the earth, against this monster from space.

5
The Iron Man's Challenge

There was no time to be wasted. The Iron Man allowed himself to be taken to pieces, arms, legs, body, head, all separate, so each part could be flown out to Australia on a different airliner.

He was too big to be flown out in one piece.

At the same time a ship sailed from China, loaded with great iron girders, and another ship sailed from Japan loaded with fuel oil. The Iron Man had ordered these. The girders and the oil and a team of engineers were unloaded on the beach of Northern Australia, near the space-bat-angel-dragon's neck. Then the Iron Man's parts were landed at the same spot, and the engineers fitted him together.

He stood up on the beach and shouted his challenge.

"Sit up," he roared. "Sit up and take notice, you great space-lizard."

The space-bat-angel-dragon sat up slowly. He had never noticed the fussing of the boats and aeroplanes down there on the beach near his neck. Now he gazed in surprise at the Iron Man, who seemed very tiny to him, though his voice was big enough.

The Iron Man spoke again.

"I challenge you," he shouted, "to a

test of strength."

A test of strength? The space-bat-angel-dragon couldn't believe his ears. A tiny little creature like the Iron Man challenging him to a test of strength? He simply laughed. Loud and long. Then he peered down again at the Iron Man, while the echo of his laugh was still rolling round the earth. He peered down out of the sky at this odd little thing on the beach, with the even tinier men scuttling around it.

"And if I can prove myself stronger

than you are, then you must promise to become my slave," cried the Iron Man.

The dragon smiled. Aircraft flew around, watching this amazing conversation between the space-bat-angel-dragon and the Iron Man. Ships out at sea watched through telescopes.

"And if you don't accept my challenge," shouted the Iron Man, "then you're a miserable cowardly reptile, not fit to bother with."

The space-bat-angel-dragon was

so astounded that he agreed. Why, he thought, when this silly little creature has finished his antics, I'll just lick him up. So the monster agreed, and watched to see what the test of strength was to be. After all, if he wanted, he could flatten the Iron Man with one eyelash.

The engineers had fastened all the girders together in the shape of a grid, a huge iron bed the size of a house. Under this they had made a steel-lined pit. Now they poured fuel oil into the pit. The space-bat-angel-dragon watched.

Now they lit the fuel oil and the flames roared up fiercely through the bars of the grid.

And now the space-bat-angel-dragon got his first shock. The Iron Man was stretching himself out on his back, on the grid, among the flames, his ankles crossed, his hands folded behind his head – just as if he were in bed, while the flames raged under and around him.

The monster stared down, and the Iron Man smiled up out of the midst of the flames.

The flames became fiercer. The grid became red-hot. The Iron Man's hair and elbows and toes became red-hot. His body became first blue, then black, then began to glow dully. He was getting red-hot. Still he smiled up at the monster, and still the flames grew fiercer.

And now the Iron Man was entirely red-hot. Pretty soon, he was almost white-hot. And still he smiled, out of white-hot eyes and with white-hot lips. And all the time the space-bat-angel-dragon stared down in astonishment.

But now the fuel oil was all burned away. Suddenly the flames died, flickered and went out. The white-hot Iron Man sat up, stood up, got stiffly off his glowing bed and began to walk to and fro on the sand, cooling. He cooled slowly. He went from white to orange, from orange to red, red to black, as he walked, coolly swinging his arms.

Now at last he spoke to the monster.

"If you can't bear to be made red-hot like me, then you are weaker than I am, and I have won, and you are my slave."

The monster began to laugh.

"All right," he roared. "Build the fire, and I'll lie on it."

He laughed again. He knew the Iron Man couldn't build a fire the size of Australia. But then his laugh stopped.

The Iron Man was pointing upwards, at the sun.

"There is the fire for you," he shouted. "You go and lie there. Go and lie on the sun till you are red-hot."

The monster gazed up at the sun. He felt strangely cold suddenly. But how could he refuse? All right! And he set off.

With slow giant wingbeats, he lifted his immense body off the earth, and flew slowly up towards the sun, while the whole earth watched . . .

Slowly he covered the distance, getting smaller and smaller as he went. At last he landed, a ragged black shape sprawled across the sun. Everybody watched. And now they saw the monster begin to glow. Blue at first, then red, then orange. Finally his shape was invisible, the same blazing white as the sun itself. The monster was white-hot on the sun.

Then they saw him returning, a blazing shape tearing itself off the sun. This shape became red as it flew.

It was writhing and growing larger. Slowly once more it became the black bat-winged shape of the dragon flying back to earth, down and down, bigger and bigger, cooling as he came, until

BUMP!!!!

He landed – this time much more heavily than before, on Australia. He landed so heavily that all over the world bells tumbled out of church towers and birds'-eggs were jarred out of their nests. The monster stared down at the Iron Man.

But it was hardly the same monster! His horns drooped, his face was wizened and black, his claws were scorched blunt, his crest flopped over limply and great ragged holes were burned in his wings. It had been terrible for him on the fires of the sun. But he had done it, and here he was. The fires of the sun are far, far hotter than any fires here on earth can ever be.

"There," he roared. "I've done it."

The Iron Man nodded. But his answer was to signal to the engineers. Once more they poured oil into the trough under the grid. Once more they lit it.

Once more the flames roared up and the black smoke billowed up into the clear blue. And once more the Iron Man stretched himself out on the grid of the raging furnace.

The space-bat-angel-dragon watched in horror. He knew what this meant for him. He would have to go once more into the sun's flames.

And now the Iron Man's hair and toes and elbows were red-hot. He lay back in the flames, smiling up at the dragon. And his whole body was becoming red-hot, then orange, and finally white, like the blazing wire inside an electric bulb.

At this point, the Iron Man was terribly afraid. For what would happen if the flames went on getting fiercer and fiercer? He would melt. He would melt and drip into the flames like so much treacle and that would be the end of him. So even though he grinned up at the dragon as though he were enjoying the flames, he was not enjoying them at all, and he was very very frightened.

Even the engineers, who were hiding behind thick asbestos screens over a mile away along the beach, felt the hair singeing on their heads, and they too thought it was the end of the Iron Man. Perhaps they had poured in just a bit too much fuel oil.

But at that very moment, and the very second that the edge of the Iron Man's ear started to melt, the fuel was used up and the flames died. The engineers came running down the beach. They saw the red-hot Iron Man getting off his fearful bed, and they saw him moving to and fro on the sand, cooling off.

At last, the Iron Man looked up at the dragon. He could hardly speak after his ordeal in the flames. Instead, he simply pointed towards the sun, and jabbed his finger towards the sun, as he gazed up at the monster.

"That's twice," he managed to say. "Now it's your turn."

The monster did not laugh. He set off, up from the earth, beating his colossal wings, writhing his long ponderous body up into the sky towards the sun. Now it was his turn. And he did not laugh. Last time had been too dreadful. But he went. He couldn't let the Iron Man win.

He couldn't let the Iron Man of the earth beat him in this terrible contest.

And so all the telescopes and cameras of the world watched him flying into the sun. They saw him land among the flames, as before. As before, they saw his great ragged shape like an ink-blot sprawled over the centre of the sun. They saw him begin to glow red, then orange. And at last they could no longer see him. He and the sun were one blinding whiteness.

He had done it again! But was the

sun burning him up? Had he melted in the sun? Where was he?

No, here he was, here he came. Slowly, slowly, down through space. Much more slowly than before. His white-hot flying body cooled slowly to red as he came, and as he grew larger, coming nearer, he finally became once more black. And the great black shape flagged its way down through space until

BUMP!!!!!!

Heavier than ever, he landed on Australia. This time the bump was so heavy, it knocked down certain sky-scrapers, sent tidal waves sweeping into harbours, and threw herds of cows on to their backs. All over the world, anybody who happened to be riding a bicycle at that moment instantly fell off. The space-bat-angel-dragon landed so ponderously because he was exhausted. And now he was a very changed monster. The fires of the sun had worked on him in a way that was awful to see. His wings were only rags of what they had been. His skin was crisped. And all his fatness had been changed by the fires of the sun into precious stones – jewels, emeralds, rubies, turquoises, and substances that had never been found on earth. And when he landed, with such a jolt, these loads of precious gems burst through the holes scorched in his skin and scattered down on to the Australian desert beneath.

But the Iron Man could not allow

himself to pity the space-bat-angel-dragon. He signalled to the engineers.

"Round three," he shouted.

And the engineers began to pour in the oil. But what was this? An enormous whoofing sound. A booming, wheezing, sneezing sound. The space-bat-angel-dragon was weeping. If the Iron Man got on to his furnace again, it would mean that he, the monster, would have to take another roasting in the sun – and he could not stand another.

"Enough, enough, enough!" he roared.

"No, no," replied the Iron Man. "I feel like going on. We've only had two each."

"It's enough," cried the dragon. "It's too much. I can't stand another. The fires of the sun are too terrible for me. I submit."

"Then I've won," shouted the Iron Man. "Because I'm quite ready to roast myself red-hot again. If you daren't, then I've won."

"You've won, yes, you've won, and I am your slave," cried the space-bat-angel-dragon. "I'll do anything you like, but not the sun again."

And he plunged his chin in the Pacific, to cool it.

"Very well," said the Iron Man. "From now on you are the slave of the earth. What can you do?"

"Alas," said the space-bat-angel-dragon, "I am useless. Utterly useless. All we do in space is fly, or make music."

"Make music?" asked the Iron Man. "How? What sort of music?"

"Haven't you heard of the music of the spheres?" asked the dragon. "It's the music that space makes to itself. All the spirits inside all the stars are singing. I'm a star spirit. I sing too. The music of the spheres is what makes space so peaceful."

"Then whatever made you want to eat up the earth?" asked the Iron Man. "If you're all so peaceful up there, how did you get such greedy and cruel ideas?"

The dragon was silent for a long time after this question. And at last he said: "It just came over me. I don't know why. It just came over me, listening to the battling shouts and the war-cries of the earth – I got excited, I wanted to join in."

"Well, you can sing for us instead," said the Iron Man. "It's a long time since anybody here on earth heard the music of the spheres. It might do us all good."

And so it was fixed. The space-bat-angel-dragon was to send his star back into the constellation of Orion, and he was to live inside the moon. And every night he was to fly around the earth, through the heavens, singing.

So his fearful shape, slowly swimming through the night sky, didn't frighten people, because it was dark and he couldn't be seen. But the whole world could hear him, a strange soft music that seemed to fill the whole of space, a deep weird singing, like millions of voices singing together.

Meanwhile the Iron Man was the world's hero. He went back to his scrap-yard. But now everybody in the world sent him a present. Some only sent him a nail. Some sent him an old car. One rich man even sent him an ocean liner. He sprawled there in his yard, chewing away, with his one ear slightly drooped where the white heat of that last roasting had slightly melted it. As he chewed, he hummed in harmony to the singing of his tremendous slave in heaven.

And the space-bat-angel's singing had the most unexpected effect. Suddenly the world became wonderfully peaceful. The singing got inside everybody and made them as peaceful as starry space, and blissfully above all their earlier little squabbles. The strange soft eerie space-music began to alter all the people of the world. They stopped making weapons. The countries began to think how they could live pleasantly alongside each other, rather than how to get rid of each other. All they wanted to do was to have peace to enjoy this strange, wild, blissful music from the giant singer in space.